There is No Point
of No Return

There is No Point
of No Return

ARNE NAESS

PENGUIN BOOKS — GREEN IDEAS

PENGUIN BOOKS

UK | USA | Canada | Ireland | Australia
India | New Zealand | South Africa

Penguin Books is part of the Penguin Random House group of companies
whose addresses can be found at global.penguinrandomhouse.com.

'The Deep Ecology Movement' first published in A. Drengson & H. Glasser (Eds.),
Selected Works of Arne Naess, X (pp. 33–55). Dordrecht, the Netherlands: Springer.
This article was first published in 1986 in *Philosophical Inquiry*, 8, 10–31.
All other essays from *Ecology of Wisdom*, published in Penguin Classics 2016
This selection published in Penguin Books 2021

001

Set in 11.5/14pt Dante MT Std
Typeset by Jouve (UK), Milton Keynes
Printed and bound in Great Britain by Clays Ltd, Elcograf S.p.A.

The authorized representative in the EEA is Penguin Random House Ireland,
Morrison Chambers, 32 Nassau Street, Dublin D02 YH68

A CIP catalogue record for this book is available from the British Library

ISBN: 978–0–241–51461–0

www.greenpenguin.co.uk

Contents

The Deep Ecology Movement

What Is Deep Ecology?

One should not expect much from definitions of movements – think of terms such as *conservatism, liberalism,* and *feminism.* Moreover, it is not necessary that supporters adhere to exactly the same definition. In what follows, a set of principles, or key terms and phrases, agreed upon by George Sessions and myself, are tentatively proposed as basic to deep ecology.*

---

* I cannot here do justice to the many authors who have contributed to the understanding of the emerging deep ecology movement. Only three will be mentioned. The newsletters written by George Sessions, Department of Philosophy, Sierra College, Rocklin, CA, are indispensable. There are six letters, April 1976, May 1979, April 1981, May 1982, May 1983, and May 1984, about 140 pages in all. The significant contributions by poets and artists are fully recognized. Most of these materials are summarized in Sessions, 1981. Bill Devall provides a short survey, in part historical, in his potent article 'The deep ecology movement' (1980). See also Devall and Sessions, 1985. Finally, The Trumpeter: Journal of Ecosophy was started in 1983 by

1. The well-being and flourishing of human and nonhuman life on Earth have value in themselves (synonyms: intrinsic value, inherent value). These values are independent of the usefulness of the nonhuman world for human purposes.

2. Richness and diversity of life-forms contribute to the relation of these values and are also values in themselves.

3. Human beings have no right to reduce this richness and diversity except to satisfy vital needs.

4. The flourishing of human life and cultures is compatible with a substantial decrease of the human population. The flourishing of nonhuman life requires such a decrease.

5. Current human interference with the nonhuman world is excessive, and the situation is rapidly worsening.

6. Policies must therefore be changed. These policies affect basic economic, technological, and ideological structures. The resulting state of affairs will be deeply different from the present state of affairs.

Alan Drengson. It was published as a print journal for fourteen years and is now an online journal.

7. The ideological change is mainly that of appreciating life quality (dwelling in situations of inherent value) rather than adhering to an increasingly higher standard of living. There will be a profound awareness of the difference between big and great.

8. Those who subscribe to the foregoing points have an obligation directly or indirectly to try to implement the necessary changes. It is this principle that highlights the importance of *deep questioning* as the process by which to follow/develop/enact the other principles.

Basic Principle 1

Formulation 1 refers to the biosphere or, more accurately, to the ecosphere as a whole. This includes individuals, species, populations, and habitats, as well as human and nonhuman cultures. From our current knowledge of all-pervasive intimate relationships, this implies a fundamental deep concern and respect. Ecological processes on the planet should, on the whole, remain intact. 'The world environment should remain 'natural'' (Gary Snyder). The term *life* is used here in a comprehensive, nontechnical way to refer also to what biologists classify as 'nonliving': rivers (watersheds), landscapes, ecosystems. For supporters of deep ecology, slogans such as 'Let the river live' illustrate this broader usage so common in most cultures. Inherent value, as used in formulation 1, is common in deep ecology literature. 'The presence of inherent value in a natural object is independent of any awareness, interest, or appreciation of it by any conscious being.'*

Basic Principle 2

More technically, formulation 2 concerns diversity and complexity. From an ecological standpoint, complexity and symbiosis are conditions for maximizing diversity. So-called simple, lower, or primitive species of plants and animals contribute essentially to richness and diversity of life. They have value in themselves and are not merely steps toward the so-called higher or rational life-forms. The second principle presupposes that life itself, as a process over evolutionary time, implies an increase of diversity and richness. The refusal to acknowledge that some life-forms have

---

* Regan, T. (1981). The nature and possibility of an environmental ethics. Environmental Ethics, 3, p. 30.

greater or lesser intrinsic value than others (see points 1 and 2) runs counter to the formulations of some ecological philosophers and New Age writers. Complexity, as referred to here, is different from complication. Urban life may be more complicated than life in a natural setting without being more complex in the sense of multifaceted quality.

Basic Principle 3

The term *vital need* is left deliberately vague in formulation 3 to allow for considerable latitude in judgment. Differences in climate and related factors, together with differences in the structures of societies as they now exist, need to be considered. (For some Inuits, snowmobiles are necessary today to satisfy vital needs; the same cannot be said for tourists.)

Basic Principle 4

People in the materially richest countries cannot be expected to reduce their excessive interference with the nonhuman world to a moderate level overnight. The stabilization and reduction of the human population will take time. Interim strategies need to be developed. In no way, however, does this excuse the current complacency. The extreme seriousness of our situation must first be realized, and the longer we wait the more drastic will be the measures needed. Until deep changes are made, substantial decreases in richness and diversity are liable to occur: the rate of extinction of species will be ten to one hundred times greater than at any other period in Earth's history.

Basic Principle 5

Formulation 5 is mild. For a realistic assessment of the situation, see the unabridged version of the IUCN's *World Conservation Strategy*. There are other works to be highly recommended, such as Gerald Barney's *Global 2000 Report to the President of the United States*. The slogan of 'noninterference' does not imply that human beings should not modify some ecosystems as do other species. Human beings have modified the earth and will probably continue to do so. At issue is the nature and extent of such interference. The fight to preserve and extend areas of wilderness or near-wilderness should continue and should focus on the general ecological functions of these areas. One such function is that large wilderness areas are required in the biosphere to allow for continued evolutionary speciation of animals and plants. Most currently designated wilderness areas and game preserves are not large enough to allow for such speciation.

Basic Principle 6

Economic growth as conceived and implemented today by the industrial states is incompatible principles 1–5. There is only a faint resemblance between ideal sustainable forms of economic growth and current policies of the industrial societies. Moreover, 'sustainable' still means 'sustainable in relation to people.' Present-day ideology tends to value things because they are scarce and because they have a commodity value. There is prestige in vast consumption and waste (to mention only several relevant factors). Whereas 'self-determination,' 'local community,' and 'think globally, act locally' will remain key terms in the ecology of human societies, nevertheless the implementation of deep changes requires increasingly global action, action across borders. Governments in developing countries are mostly uninterested in deep ecological issues. When the governments of industrial societies try to promote ecological measures through these governments, practically nothing is accomplished (for example, with problems of desertification). Given this situation, support for global action through nongovernmental international organizations becomes increasingly important. Many of these organizations are able to act globally 'from grass roots to grass roots,' thus avoiding negative governmental interference. Cultural diversity today requires advanced technology, that is, techniques that advance the basic goals of each culture. So-called soft, intermediate, and alternative technologies are steps in this direction.

Basic Principle 7

Some economists criticize the term *quality of life* because, they say, it is vague. On closer inspection, however, what they consider to be vagueness is actually the non-quantitative nature of the term. One cannot quantify adequately what is important for quality of life as discussed here, and there is no need to do so.

Basic Principle 8

There is ample room for different opinions about *priorities*: what should be done first, what next; what is most urgent; what is clearly necessary as opposed to highly desirable but not absolutely pressing. Although many supporters of the deep ecology movement may find the above formulations useful, others will certainly feel that they are imperfect, even misleading. If they need to formulate in a few words what is basic in deep ecology, they will propose an alternative set of sentences. I shall, of course, be glad to refer to those formulations as alternatives. There ought to be a measure of diversity in what is considered basic and common. Should we call the movement the deep ecology movement?* There are at least six other designations that cover most of the same issues: 'Ecological Resistance,' used by John Rodman in important discussions; 'The New Natural Philosophy,' coined by Joseph Meeker; 'Eco-philosophy,' used by Sigmund Kvaløy and others to emphasize (1) a

---

* I proposed the name Deep, Long Range Ecology Movement in a lecture at the Third World Future Research Conference (Bucharest, September 1972). 'The shallow and the deep, long-range ecology movement: A summary.' (Naess, 1973) is a summary of that lecture. Adherents of the deep ecology movement fairly commonly use the term deep ecologist, whereas shallow ecologist, I am glad to say, is rather uncommon. Both terms may be considered arrogant and slightly misleading. I prefer to use the awkward but more egalitarian expression 'supporter of the deep (or shallow) ecology movement,' avoiding personification. Also, it is common to call deep ecology consistently antianthropocentric. This has led to misconceptions: see my 'A defense of the deep ecology movement' (1984).

highly critical assessment of industrial growth societies from a general ecological point of view and (2) the ecology of the human species; 'Green Philosophy and Politics' (although the term *green* is often used in Europe, in the United States it has a misleading association with the rather 'blue' Green Revolution); 'Sustainable Earth Ethics,' as used by G. Tyler Miller; and 'Ecosophy,' eco-wisdom, which is my own favorite term. Others could also be mentioned. Why use the adjective *deep*? This question will be easier to answer after the contrast is made between shallow and deep ecological concerns. What I am talking about is not a philosophy in any academic sense, nor is it institutionalized as a religion. It is better described as *nonanthropocentric*. Various persons come together in campaigns and direct actions. They form a circle of friends supporting the same kind of lifestyle, which others term 'simple' but they themselves think is rich and many-sided. They agree on a vast array of political issues, although they may otherwise support different political parties. As in all social movements, slogans and rhetoric are indispensable for in-group coherence. They react together against the same threats in a predominantly nonviolent way. Perhaps the most influential participants are artists and writers who do not articulate their insights in terms of professional philosophy, but do express themselves in art or poetry. For these reasons, I use the term *move-ment* rather than *philosophy*.

Deep Versus Shallow Ecology

A number of key terms and slogans from the environmental debate will clarify the contrast between the shallow and the deep ecology movements.

Pollution

Shallow approach: Technology seeks to purify the air and water and to spread pollution more evenly. Laws limit permissible pollution. Polluting industries are preferably exported to developing countries.

Deep approach: Pollution is evaluated from a biospheric point of view*, not centring on its effects on human health, but on life as a whole, including life conditions

---

* The technical term biospheric should perhaps be avoided because it favors the scientifically fruitful distinction between biosphere and ecosphere. I use the term life in a broad sense common in everyday speech, and may therefore speak of landscapes and larger systems of the ecosphere as 'living' – ultimately speaking of the life of the planet. The biospheric point of view referred to in the text is not a

of every species and system. The shallow reaction to acid rain is to avoid action by demands for more research, demands to find species of trees tolerating high acidity, and so on, whereas the deep approach concentrates on what is going on in the total ecosystem and asks for a high-priority fight against the economy and technology responsible for acid rain. The priority is to fight deep causes of pollution, not merely the superficial, short-range effects. The developing world cannot afford to pay the total cost of the war against pollution, and consequently require the assistance of the developed world. Exporting pollution is not only a crime against humanity, but also against life.

Resources

Shallow approach: The emphasis is on resources for human beings, especially the present generation in affluent societies. In this view, the Earth's resources belong to those who have the technology to exploit them. There is confidence that resources will not be depleted because, as they get rarer, a high market price will conserve them, and substitutes will be

---

narrower point of view than the ecospheric because bios is used in a broad sense.

found through technological progress. Further, animals, plants, and natural objects are valuable only as resources for human beings. If no human use is known, they can be destroyed with indifference.

Deep approach: The concern here is with resources and habitat for all life-forms for their own sake. No natural object is conceived of solely as a resource. This then leads to a critical evaluation of human modes of production and consumption. One must ask, To what extent does an increase here favour ultimate values in human life? To what extent does it satisfy vital needs, locally and globally? How can economic, legal, and educational institutions be changed to counteract destructive increases? How can resource use serve the quality of life rather than the economic standard of living as generally promoted in consumerism? There is an emphasis here on an *ecosystem approach* rather than just the consideration of isolated life-forms or local situations. There is a long-range maximal perspective of time and place.

Population

Shallow approach: The threat of (human) overpopulation is seen mainly as a problem for developing countries. One condones or even cheers population increases in one's own country for short-sighted economic, military, or other reasons; an increase in the number of human beings is considered a value in itself or as economically profitable. The issue of optimum population for humankind is discussed without reference to the question of the optimum population of other life-forms. The destruction of wild habitats caused by an increasing human population is accepted as an inevitable evil. Drastic decreases of wild life-forms tend to be accepted as long as species are not driven to extinction. Animal social relations are ignored. The long-term substantial reduction of the global human population is not seen as a desired goal. One has a right to defend one's own borders against 'illegal aliens,' no matter what the population pressures elsewhere.

Deep approach: It is recognized that excessive pressures on planetary life conditions stem from the human population explosion. The pressure stemming from industrial societies is a major factor, and population reduction must have a high priority in those societies, as well as in developing countries. Estimates of an optimal human population vary. Some quantitative estimates are 100 million, 500 million, and 1,000 million, but it is recognized that there must be a long-range human-population reduction through mild but tenacious political and economic measures. This will make possible, as a result of increased habitat, population growth for thousands of species that are now constrained by human pressures.

Cultural Diversity And Appropriate Technology

Shallow approach: Industrialization of the kind manifested in the West is held to be the goal for developing countries. The universal adoption of Western technology is compatible with mild cultural diversity and the conservation of good (from the Western point of view) elements in present-day non-industrial societies. There is a low estimate of deep cultural differences that deviate significantly from Western standards.

Deep approach: Cultural diversity is an analogue on the human level to the biological richness and diversity of life-forms. We should give high priority to cultural anthropology in education in industrial societies. We should limit the impact of Western technology on nonindustrial countries and defend the developing world against foreign domination. Political and economic policies should favor subcultures within industrialized societies. Local, soft technologies will allow a basic cultural assessment of any technical innovations. The deep approach freely criticizes so-called advanced technology and concepts of 'progress.'

Land And Sea Ethics

Shallow approach: Landscapes, ecosystems, rivers, and other wholes of nature are cut into fragments; larger units and gestalts are disregarded. These fragments are regarded as the property and resources of individuals, organizations, or states. Conservation is argued in terms of 'multiple use' and 'cost-benefit analysis.' Social costs and long-term ecological costs are not included. Wildlife management conserves nature for 'future generations of human beings.' The erosion of soils or of groundwater quality is noted as a human loss, but a strong belief in future technological progress makes deep changes seem unnecessary.

Deep approach: Earth does not belong to human beings. The Norwegian landscapes, rivers, fauna and flora, and the surrounding sea are not the property of Norwegians. Human beings only inhabit the land, using resources to satisfy vital needs. If their non-vital needs conflict with the vital needs of nonhuman life-forms, human beings might yield. The destruction now going on will not be cured by a technological fix. Current arrogant notions in industrial (and other) societies must be resisted.

Education And Scientific Enterprise

Shallow approach: The degradation of the environment and resource depletion necessitate the further training of experts who can advise on how to combine economic growth with the maintenance of a healthy environment. We are likely to need highly manipulative technology when global economic growth makes further degradation inevitable. The scientific enterprise must continue giving priority to the 'hard' sciences. This necessitates high educational standards with intense competition in relevant 'tough' areas of learning.

Deep approach: Education should concentrate on increased sensitivity to non-consumptive goods and on such consumables as we have enough of for all, provided sane ecological policies are adopted. Education will therefore counteract the excessive valuation of things with a price tag. There should be a shift in emphasis from 'hard' to 'soft' sciences, especially those that stress local culture and global cooperation.

The educational objective of the *World Conservation Strategy*, 'building support for conservation,' should be accorded priority within the deeper framework of respect for the biosphere. In the future, there will be no shallow movement, if shallow policies are increasingly adopted by governments and, thus, need no support from a special social movement.

Why A 'Deep' Ecology?

The decisive difference between a shallow and a deep ecology movement hinges on the willingness to question, and to appreciate the importance of questioning, every economic and political policy in public. The questioning is 'deep' and public. It asks *why* more insistently and consistently, taking nothing for granted.

Deep ecology can readily admit the practical effectiveness of anthropocentric arguments. 'It is essential for conservation to be seen as central to human interests and aspirations. At the same time, people – from heads of state to the members of rural communities – will most readily be brought to demand conservation if they themselves recognize the contribution of conservation to the achievement of their needs, as perceived by them, and the solution of their problems, as perceived by them' (IUCN 1980, sec. 13). Since most policies serving the biosphere also serve humanity in the long run, they may, at least initially, be accepted on the basis of narrow 'anthropocentric' arguments. Nevertheless, such a tactical approach has significant limitations. There are three dangers. First, some policies based on successful anthropocentric arguments turn out to violate or compromise unduly the objectives of deeper argumentation. Second, the strong motivation to fight for decisive change and the willingness to serve a great cause are weakened; and, third, the complicated arguments in human-centered conservation documents such as the *World Conservation Strategy* go beyond the time and ability of many people to assimilate and understand and also tend to interminable technical disagreements among experts. Special interest groups with narrow, short-term exploitative objectives that run counter to saner eco-policies often exploit these disagreements and thereby stall the debate and steps toward effective action.

When arguing from deep ecological premises, one need not discuss at all most of the complicated proposed technological fixes. The relative merits of alternative-technology proposals in industrial societies concerned with how to increase energy production are pointless if our vital needs have already been met. The focus on vital issues activates mental energy and strengthens motivation. The shallow environmental approach, on the other hand, tends to make the human population more passive and less interested in environmental issues. The deep ecology movement tries to clarify the fundamental presuppositions underlying our economic approach in terms of value priorities, philosophy, and religion. In the shallow movement, argument comes to a halt long before this. The deep ecology movement is therefore 'the ecology movement that questions deeper.'

Self-Realization: An Ecological Approach to Being in the World

Humanity has struggled, for about 2,500 years, with basic questions about who we are, where we are headed, and the nature of the reality in which we are included. This is a short period in the lifetime of a species, and an even shorter time in the history of the earth, to which we belong as mobile beings. I am not capable of saying very new things in answer to these questions, but I can look at them from a *somewhat* different angle, using somewhat different conceptual tools and images.

What I am going to say, more or less in my own way and in that of my friends, can be condensed roughly into the following points:

1. We underestimate ourselves. And I emphasize *selves*. We tend to confuse our 'self' with the narrow ego.

2. Human nature is such that, with sufficient comprehensive maturity, we cannot help but

identify ourselves with all living beings, beautiful or ugly, big or small, sentient or not. The adjective *comprehensive*, meaning 'all-sided,' as in 'comprehensive maturity,' deserves a note: Descartes seemed to be rather immature in his relationship with animals; Schopenhauer was not very advanced in his relationship to his family (kicking his mother down a staircase?); Heidegger was amateurish – to say the least – in his political behavior. Weak identification with nonhumans is compatible with maturity in some major sets of relationships, such as those toward one's family or friends. And so I use the qualification *comprehensive* to mean 'being mature in *all* major relationships.'

3. Traditionally, the *maturity of the self* has been considered to develop through three stages: from ego to social self (comprising the ego), and from social self to a metaphysical self (comprising the social self). But in this conception of the maturity of the self, nature is largely left out. Our immediate environment, our home (where we belong as children), and the identification with nonhuman living beings are largely ignored.

Therefore, I tentatively introduce, perhaps for the very first time, the concept of *ecological self*. We may be said to be in, and of, nature from the very beginning of ourselves. Society and human relationships are important, but our own self is much richer in its constitutive relationships. These relationships are not only those we have with other humans and the human community (I have elsewhere introduced the term *mixed community* to mean those communities in which we consciously and deliberately live close together with certain animals), but also those we have with other living beings.

4. The meaning of life, and the joy we experience in living, is enhanced through increased self-realization, that is, through the fulfillment of potentials that each of us has, but that are never the same for any two living beings. Whatever the differences between beings, increased self-realization implies a broadening and deepening of the self.

5. Because of an inescapable process of identification with others, with increasing maturity, the self is widened and deepened. We 'see ourselves in others.' Our self-realization is hindered if the self-realization

of others, with whom we identify, is hindered. Our self-love will fight this hindrance by assisting in the self-realization of others according to the formula 'Live and let live!' Thus, everything that can be achieved by altruism – the *dutiful, moral* consideration for others – can be achieved, and much more, by the process of widening and deepening ourselves. Following Kant, we then act *beautifully*, but neither morally nor immorally (in the sense of from duty).

6. One of the great challenges today is to save the planet from further ecological devastation, which violates both the enlightened self-interest of humans and the self-interest of nonhumans and decreases the potential of joyful existence for all.

Now, proceeding to elaborate these points, I shall start with the peculiar and fascinating terms *ego* and *self*.

The simplest answer to who or what I am is to point to my body. But clearly I cannot identify myself, or even my ego, with my body. For example, compare the following sentences:

I know Mr Smith.	My body knows Mr Smith.
I like poetry.	My body likes poetry.
The only difference between us is that you are a Presbyterian and I am a Baptist.	The only difference between our bodies is that you are a Presbyterian and I am a Baptist.

In the preceding sentences, we cannot substitute 'my body' for 'I.' Nor can we substitute 'my mind' or 'my mind and my body' for 'I.' More adequately, we may substitute 'I as a person' for 'I,' but this does not, of course, tell us what the ego or the self is.

Several thousand years of philosophical, psychological, and social-psychological thinking has not brought us any adequate conception of the *I*, the *ego*, or the *self*. In modern psychotherapy, these notions play an indispensable role, but, of course, the practical goal of therapy does not necessitate philosophical clarification of these terms. It is important to remind ourselves about the strange and marvelous phenomena with which we are dealing. Perhaps the extreme closeness and nearness of these objects of thought and reflection add to our difficulties. I shall offer only one simple sentence that resembles a definition of the ecological self: The *ecological self* of a person is that with which this person identifies.

The key sentence (rather than a definition) about the self shifts the burden of clarification from the term *self* to that of *identification*, or rather, the process of identification.

I shall continue to concentrate on the ecology of the self, but shall first say some things about identification. What would be a paradigm situation involving identification? It would be a situation that elicits intense empathy. My standard example involves a nonhuman being I met in the 1940s. I was looking through an old-fashioned microscope at the dramatic meeting of two drops of different chemicals. At that moment, a flea jumped from a lemming that was strolling along the table. The insect landed in the middle of the acid chemicals. To save it was impossible. It took minutes for the flea to die. The tiny being's movements were dreadfully expressive. Naturally, I felt a painful sense of compassion and empathy. But the empathy was *not* basic. Rather, it was a process of identification: I saw myself in the flea. If I had been *alienated* from the flea, not seeing intuitively anything even resembling myself, the death struggle would have left me feeling indifferent. So there must be identification for there to be compassion and, among humans, solidarity.

One of the authors contributing admirably to a clarification of the study of the self is Eric Fromm:

The doctrine that love for oneself is identical with 'self-ishness' and an alternative to love for others has pervaded theology, philosophy, and popular thought; the same doctrine has been rationalized in scientific language in Freud's theory of narcissism. Freud's concept presupposes a fixed amount of libido. In the infant, all of the libido has the child's own person as its objective, the stage of 'primary narcissism,' as Freud calls it. During the individual's development, the libido is shifted from one's own person toward other objects. If a person is blocked in his 'object-relationships,' the libido is withdrawn from the objects and returned to his or her own person; this is called 'secondary narcissism.' According to Freud, the more love I turn toward the outside world the less love is left for myself, and vice versa. He thus describes the phenomenon of love as an impoverishment of one's self-love because all libido is turned to an object outside oneself.

What Fromm attributes here to Freud we can now attribute to the shrinkage of self-perception implied in the fascination for ego trips. Fromm opposes such a shrinkage of self. The following quotation from Fromm concerns love of persons but, as 'ecosophers,' we find the notions of care, respect, responsibility, and knowledge applicable to living beings in the wide sense.

Love of others and love of ourselves are not alternatives. On the contrary, an attitude of love toward themselves will be found in all those who are capable of loving others. Love, in principle, is indivisible as far as the connection between 'objects' and one's own self is concerned. Genuine love is an expression of productiveness and implies care, respect, responsibility, and knowledge. It is not an 'effect' in the sense of being affected by somebody, but an active striving for the growth and happiness of the loved person, rooted in one's own capacity to love.

Fromm is very instructive about unselfishness – it is diametrically opposed to selfishness, but is still based on alienation and a narrow perception of self. We might add that what he says also applies to persons sacrificing of themselves:

The nature of unselfishness becomes particularly apparent in its effect on others and most frequently, in our culture, in the effect the 'unselfish' mother has on her children. She believes that by her unselfishness her children will experience what it means to be loved and to learn, in turn, what it means to love. The effect of her unselfishness, however, does not at all correspond to her expectations. The children do not show the happiness of persons who are convinced that they are loved; they are anxious, tense, afraid of the mother's disapproval, and anxious to live up to her expectations. Usually, they are affected by their mother's hidden hostility against life, which they sense rather than recognize, and eventually become imbued with it themselves . . .

If one has a chance to study the effect of a mother with genuine self-love, one can see that there is nothing more conducive to giving a child the experience of what love, joy, and happiness are than being loved by a mother who loves herself.

We need environmental ethics, but when people feel that they unselfishly give up, or even sacrifice, their self-interests to show love for nature, this is probably, in the long run, a treacherous basis for conservation. Through identification, they may come to see that their own interests are served by conservation, through genuine self-love, the love of a widened and deepened self.

At this point, the notion of a being's interests furnishes a bridge from self-love to self-realization. It should not surprise us that Fromm, influenced as he is by Spinoza and William James, makes use of that bridge. 'What is considered self-interest?' Fromm asks. His answer:

There are two fundamentally different approaches to this problem. One is the objectivistic approach most clearly formulated by Spinoza. To him self-interest or the interest 'to seek one's profit' is identical with virtue.

'The more,' he says, 'each person strives and is able to seek his profit, that is to say, to preserve his being, the more virtue does he possess; on the other hand, in so far as each person neglects his own profit he is impotent.' According to this view, the interest of humans is to preserve their existence, which is the same as realizing their inherent potentialities. This concept of self-interest is objectivistic inasmuch as 'interest' is not conceived in terms of the subjective feeling of what one's interest is but in terms of what the nature of a human is, 'objectively.'

'Realizing inherent potentialities' is one of the good, less-than-ten-word clarifications of 'self-realization.' The questions 'What are the inherent potentialities of the beings of species x?' and 'What are the inherent potentialities of this specimen of the species y?' obviously lead to reflections about, and studies of, x and y.

As humans we cannot just follow the impulses of the moment when asking what our inherent potentialities are. Fromm means something like this when he calls an approach 'objectivistic' as opposed to an approach 'in terms of subjective feeling.' Because of the high estimation of feeling and a correspondingly low estimate of so-called objectification (*Verdinglichung*, reification) within deep ecology, Fromm's terminology is inadequate today, but what he means to say is appropriate. And it is obviously relevant when we deal with species other than humans: Animals and plants have interests in the sense of ways of realizing inherent potentialities, which we can study only by interacting with these beings. We cannot rely on our momentary impulses, however important they are in general.

The expression 'preserve his being,' in the quotation from Spinoza, is better than 'preserve his existence,' since the latter is often associated with physical survival and a struggle for survival. An even better translation is perhaps 'persevere in his being' (*perseverare in suo esse*). This has to do with acting from one's own nature. Survival is only a necessary condition, not a sufficient condition of continued self-realization. (An act of self-realization may discontinue self-realization because it leads to immediate death. This opinion goes probably against what Spinoza would say.)

The concept of self-realization, as dependent upon insight into our own potentialities, makes it easy to see the possibilities of ignorance and misunderstanding in terms of what these potentialities are. The ego-trip interpretation of the potentialities of humans presupposes a major underestimation of the richness and broadness of our potentialities. As Fromm puts it, 'man can deceive himself about his real self-interest if he is ignorant of his self and its real needs.'

The 'everything hangs together' maxim of ecology applies to the self and its relation to other living beings, ecosystems, the ecosphere, and the earth, with its long history.

The existence and importance of the ecological self are easy to illustrate with some examples of what has happened in my own country, Norway.

The scattered human habitation along the Arctic coast of Norway is uneconomic and unprofitable, from the point of view of the current economic policy of our welfare state. The welfare norms require that every family should have a connection by telephone (in case of illness). This costs a considerable amount of money. The same holds for mail and other services. Local fisheries are largely uneconomic perhaps because a foreign armada of big trawlers of immense capacity is fishing just outside the fjords. The availability of jobs was decreasing in the mid-1980s.

The government, therefore, heavily subsidized the

resettlement of people from the Arctic wilderness, concentrating them in so-called centers of development, that is, small areas with a town at the center. But the people are clearly not the same when their bodies have been thus transported. The social, economic, *and natural setting* is now vastly different. The objects with which people work and live are completely different. There is a consequent loss of personal identity. 'Who am I?' they ask. Their self-respect, self-esteem, is impaired. What is adequate in the so-called periphery of the country is different from what counts at the so-called centers.

If people are relocated or, rather, transplanted from a steep, mountainous place to a plain, they also realize, but too late, that their home-place has been part of themselves – that they have identified with features of the place. And the way of life in the tiny locality, the density of social relations, has formed their persons. Again, they are not the same as they were.

Tragic cases can be seen in other parts of the Arctic. We all regret the fate of the Inuit, their difficulties in finding *a new identity*, a new social self, and a new, more comprehensive ecological self. The Lapps of Arctic Norway have been hurt by the diversion of a river for hydroelectricity. In court, accused of an illegal demonstration at the river, one Lapp said that the part of the river in question was 'part of himself.'

This kind of spontaneous answer is not uncommon among people. They have not heard about the philosophy of the wider and deeper self, but they talk spontaneously as if they had.

We may try to make the sentence 'This place is part of myself' more intellectually understandable by reformulations. For example, we might say, 'My relation to this place is part of myself,' or 'If this place is destroyed, something in me is destroyed,' or 'My relation to this place is such that if the place is changed, I am changed.'

One drawback with these reformulations is that they make it easy to continue thinking of two completely separable, real entities, a self and the place, joined by an external relation. The original sentence, rather, conveys the impression that there is an internal relation of sorts. I say 'of sorts,' because we must take into account that it may not be reciprocal. If I am changed, even destroyed, the place would be destroyed according to one usual interpretation of *internal relation*. From the point of phenomenology and the concrete-content view, the reciprocity holds, but that is a special interpretation. We may use an interpretation such that if we are changed, the river need not be changed.

The reformulation 'If this place is destroyed, something in me is killed' perhaps articulates some of the feelings usually felt when people see the destruction of places they deeply love or to which they have the intense feeling of belonging. Today, more space per human being is violently transformed than ever, at the same time as the number of human beings increases. The kind of 'killing' referred to occurs all over the globe, but very rarely does it lead to strong counteraction. Resignation prevails: 'You cannot stop progress.'

The newborn lacks, of course, any conceptions, however rudimentary, corresponding to the tripartition: subject, object, medium. The conception (not the concept) of one's own ego probably comes rather late, say, after the first year. A vague network of relations comes first. This network of perceived and conceived relations is neutral, fitting what in British philosophy was called *neutral monism*. In a sense, it is this basic sort of crude monism we are working out anew, not by trying to be babies again, but by better understanding our ecological self. It has not had favorable conditions of development since before the time that the Renaissance glorified our ego by putting it in some kind of opposition to the rest of reality.

What is now the practical importance of this conception of a wide and deep ecological self?

Opponents often argue that we defend nature in our rich, industrial society in order to secure beauty, recreation, sport, and other nonvital interests for ourselves. It makes us strong if, after honest reflection, we find that we feel threatened in our innermost self. If so, we more convincingly defend a *vital* interest, not only something out there. We are engaged in self-defense. And to defend fundamental *human* rights is vital self-defense.

The best introduction to the psychology of the self is still to be found in the excellent and superbly readable book *Principles of Psychology*, published in 1890 by the American psychologist and philosopher William James. His hundred-page chapter on the consciousness of self stresses the plurality of components of the wide and deep self as a complex entity. (Unfortunately, he prefers to talk about the plurality of selves. I think it may be better to talk about the plurality of the components of the wide self.)

The plurality of components can be easily illustrated by reference to the dramatic phenomenon of alternating personality. 'Any man becomes, as we say, *inconsistent* with himself if he forgets his engagements, pledges, knowledge, and habits . . . In the hypnotic trance we can easily produce an alternation of personality . . . by telling him he is an altogether imaginary personage.'

If we say that somebody is not himself or herself today, we may refer to a great many different *relations* to other people, to material things, and, certainly, to what we call his or her environment, the home, the garden, the neighborhood.

When James says that these relata *belong* to the self, it is, of course, not in the sense that the self has eaten the home, the environment, and so forth. Such an interpretation testifies that the self is still identified with the body. Nor does it mean that an *image* of the house *inside* the consciousness of the person belongs to the self. When somebody says that a part of a river landscape is part of himself or herself, we intuitively grasp roughly what the person means. But it is of course difficult to elucidate the meaning in philosophical or psychological terminology.

A last example from William James: We understand what is meant when somebody says, 'As a man I pity you, but as an official I must show you no mercy.' Obviously, the self of an official cannot empirically be defined except as a relation in a complex social setting. Thus, the self cannot possibly be inside the body or inside a consciousness.

Enough! The main point is that we do not hesitate *today*, being inspired by ecology and a revived intimate relation to nature, to recognize and accept wholeheartedly our ecological self.

The next section is rather metaphysical. I do not *defend* all the views presented in this part of my discussion. I wish primarily to inform you about them. As a student and admirer since 1930 of Gandhi's nonviolent, direct actions in bloody conflicts, I am inevitably influenced by his metaphysics, which to him personally furnished tremendously powerful motivation and which contributed to keeping him going until his death. His supreme aim was not India's *political* liberation. He led a crusade against extreme poverty, caste suppression, and terror in the name of religion. This crusade was necessary, but the liberation of the individual human being was his supreme aim. It is strange for many to listen to what he himself said about his ultimate goal: 'What I want to achieve – what I have been striving and pining to achieve these thirty years – is self-realization, to see God face to face, to attain *Moksha* (Liberation). I live and move and have my being in pursuit of that goal. All that I do by way of speaking and writing, and all my ventures in the political field, are directed to this same end.'

This sounds individualistic to the Western mind – a common misunderstanding. If the self Gandhi is speaking about were the ego or the 'narrow' self (*jiva*) of egocentric interest, the 'ego trips,' why then work for the poor? It is for him the supreme or universal Self – the *Atman* – that is to be realized. Paradoxically, it seems, he tries to reach self-realization through *selfless action*, that is, through the reduction of the dominance of the narrow self or the ego. Through the wider Self, every living being is connected intimately, and from this intimacy follows the capacity of *identification* and, as its natural consequences, practice of nonviolence. No moralizing is needed, just as we do not need morals to breathe. We need to cultivate our insight: The rock-bottom foundation of the technique for achieving the power of nonviolence is belief in the essential oneness of all life.

Historically, we have seen how nature conservation is nonviolent at its very core. Gandhi says: 'I believe in *advaita* (nonduality), I believe in the essential unity of man and, for that matter, of all that lives. Therefore I believe that if one man gains spirituality, the whole world gains with him and, if one man fails, the whole world fails to that extent.'

Surprisingly enough, Gandhi was extreme in his personal consideration for the self-realization of living beings other than humans. When traveling, he brought a goat with him to satisfy his need for milk. This was part of a nonviolent demonstration against certain cruel features in Hindu ways of milking cows. Furthermore, some European companions who lived with Gandhi in his ashrams were taken aback that he let snakes, scorpions, and spiders move unhindered into their bedrooms – animals fulfilling their lives. He even prohibited people from having a stock of medicines against poisonous bites. He believed in the possibility of satisfactory coexistence, and he proved right. There were no accidents. Ashram people would naturally look into their shoes for scorpions before using them. Even when moving over the floor in darkness, one could easily avoid trampling on one's fellow beings. Thus, Gandhi recognized a basic, common right to live and blossom, to self-realization in a wide sense applicable to any being that can be said to have interests or needs.

Gandhi made manifest the internal relation between self-realization, nonviolence, and what sometimes has been called biospherical egalitarianism.

In the environment in which I grew up, I heard that what is serious in life is to get *to be* somebody – to outdo others in something, being victorious in a comparison of abilities. What makes this conception of the meaning and goal of life especially dangerous today is the vast, international economic competition. Free market, perhaps, yes, but the law of supply and demand of separate, isolatable 'goods and services,' independent of needs, must not be made to reign over increasing other areas of our life.

The ability to cooperate, to work with people, to make them feel good, *pays*, of course, in a fiercely individualist society, and high positions may require this, but only as long as, ultimately, it is subordinated to the career, to the basic norms of the ego trip, not to a self-realization beyond the ego.

To identify self-realization with the ego trip manifests a vast underestimation of the human self.

According to a common translation of Pali or Sanskrit texts, Buddha taught his disciples that the human mind should embrace all living things as a mother cares for her son, her only son. Some of you who never would feel it meaningful or possible that a human *self* could embrace all living things might stick to the usual translation. We shall then only ask that your *mind* embraces all living beings and that your good intention is to care and feel and act with compassion.

If the Sanskrit word translated into English is *Atman*, it is instructive to note that this term has the basic meaning of 'self,' rather than 'mind' or 'spirit,' as you see in translations. The superiority of the translation using the word 'self' stems from the consideration that if your *self* in the wide sense embraces another being, you need no moral exhortation to show care. Surely, you care for yourself without feeling any moral pressure to do it – provided you have not succumbed to a neurosis of some kind, developing self-destructive tendencies or hating yourself.

Incidentally, the Australian ecological feminist Patsy Hallen uses a formula close to that of Buddha: We are here to embrace rather than conquer the world. It is of interest to notice that the term 'world' is used here, rather than 'living beings.' I suspect that our thinking need not proceed from the notion of living being to that of the world, but we will conceive reality or the world we live in as alive in a wide, not easily defined sense. There will then be no nonliving beings to care for.

If self-realization or self-fulfillment is today habitually associated with lifelong ego trips, isn't it stupid to use this term for self-realization in the widely different sense of Gandhi or, less religiously loaded, as a term for widening and deepening your self so that it embraces all life-forms? Perhaps it is. But I think the very popularity of the term makes people listen for a moment, feeling safe. In that moment, the notion of a greater self should be introduced to show that if people equate self-realization with ego trips, they seriously *underestimate* themselves. 'You are much greater, deeper, generous, and capable of more dignity and joy than you think! A wealth of noncompetitive joy is open to you!'

But I have another important reason for inviting people to think in terms of deepening and widening their *self*, starting with the ego trip as a crudest, but inescapable, point zero. It has to do with a notion usually placed as the opposite of the egoism of the ego trip, namely, the notion of *altruism*. The Latin term *ego* has as its opposite the *alter*. Altruism implies that *ego* sacrifices its interest in favor of the other, the *alter*. The motivation is primarily that of duty: It is said that we *ought* to love others as strongly as we love ourselves.

Unfortunately, humankind is very limited in what it can love from mere duty or, more generally, from moral exhortation. From the Renaissance to World War II, about four hundred cruel wars were fought by Christian nations for the flimsiest of reasons. It seems to me that in the future, more emphasis has to be given to the conditions under which we most naturally widen and deepen our self. With a sufficiently wide and deep self, *ego* and *alter* as opposites are eliminated stage by stage. The distinction is in a way transcended.

Early in life, the social self is sufficiently developed so that we do not prefer to eat a big cake alone. We share the cake with our friends and our nearest. We identify with these people sufficiently to see our joy in their joy and to see our disappointment in theirs.

Now is the time *to share* with all life on our maltreated earth through the deepening identification with life-forms and the greater units, the ecosystems, and Gaia, the fabulous, old planet of ours.

Immanuel Kant introduced a pair of contrasting concepts that deserve to be extensively used in our effort to live harmoniously in, for, and of nature: the concepts of the *moral act* and the *beautiful act*.

Moral acts are those motivated by the intention to follow the moral laws, at whatever cost, that is, to do our moral duty solely out of respect for that duty. Therefore, the supreme *test* of our success in performing a pure, moral act is that we do it completely against our inclination, that we, so to say, hate to do it, but are compelled by our respect for the moral law. Kant was deeply awed by two phenomena, 'the heaven with its stars above me and the moral law within me.'

But if we do something we should do according to a moral law, but do it out of inclination and with pleasure – what then? Should we then abstain or try to work up some displeasure? Not at all, according to Kant. If we do what morals say is right because of positive inclination, then we perform a *beautiful* act. Now, my point is that in environmental affairs, perhaps we should try primarily to influence people toward beautiful acts. Work on their inclinations rather than morals. Unhappily, the extensive moralizing within environmentalism has given the public the false impression that we primarily ask them to sacrifice, to show more responsibility, more concern, better morals. As I see it, we need the immense variety of sources of joy opened through increased sensitivity toward the richness and diversity of life and the landscapes of free nature. We all can contribute to this individually, but it is also a question of politics, local and global. Part of the joy stems from the consciousness of our intimate relation to something bigger than our ego, something that has endured through millions of years and is worthy of continued life for millions of years. The requisite care flows naturally if the self is widened and deepened so that protection of free nature is felt and conceived as protection of ourselves.

Academically speaking, what I suggest is the supremacy of environmental ontology and realism over environmental ethics as a means of invigorating the environmental movement in the years to come. If reality is experienced by the ecological self, our behavior *naturally* and beautifully follows norms of strict environmental ethics. We certainly need to hear about our ethical shortcomings from time to time, but we more easily change through encouragement and through a deepened perception of reality and our own self. That is, deepened realism. How is this to be brought about? The question lies outside the scope of this essay! It is more a question of community therapy than community science: healing our relations to the widest community, that of all living beings.

The subtitle of this essay is 'An Ecological Approach

to Being in the World.' I am now going to discuss a little about 'nature,' with all the qualities we spontaneously experience, as identical with the reality we live in. That means a movement from being in the world to being in nature. Then, finally, I shall ask for the goal or purpose of being in the world.

Is joy in the subject? I would say no. Joy is just as much or as little *in* the object. The joy of a joyful tree is primarily *in* the tree, we should say – if we are pressed to make a choice between the two possibilities. But we should not be pressed. There is a third position. The joy is a feature of the *indivisible*, concrete unit of subject, object, and medium. In a sense, self-realization involves experiences of the infinitely rich, joyful aspect of reality. It is misleading, according to my intuition, to locate joy inside my consciousness. What is joyful is something that is not subjective; joy is an attribute of a reality wider than a conscious ego. This is philosophically how I contribute to the explanation of the internal relation between joy, happiness, and human self-realization. But this conceptual exercise is mainly of interest to an academic philosopher. What I am driving at is probably something that may be suggested with less conceptual gymnastics: It is unwarranted to believe that how we feel nature to be is not like how nature really is. It is rather that reality is so rich that we cannot see everything at once, but separate parts or aspects in separate moods. The joyful tree I see in the morning light is not the sorrowful one I see in the night, even if, in their abstract structure, they (physically) are the same.

It is very human to ask for the ultimate goal or purpose of being in the world. This may be a misleading way of framing a question. It may seem to suggest that the goal or purpose must somehow lie outside or beyond the world. Perhaps this can be avoided by living out 'in the world.' It is characteristic of our time that we subjectivize and individualize the question asked of each of us: What do you consider the ultimate goal or purpose for *your* life? Or, we leave out the question of priorities and simply ask for goals and purposes.

The main title of this essay is partly motivated by the conviction that *self-realization* is an adequate key-term expression one uses to answer the question of ultimate goal. It is of course only a key term. An answer by a philosopher can scarcely be shorter than the little book *Ethics* by Spinoza.

To understand the function of the term *self-realization* in this capacity, it is useful to compare it with two others, *pleasure* and *happiness*. The first suggests hedonism, the second eudaemonism in a professional philosophical, but just as vague and ambiguous, jargon. Both terms broadly connote states of feeling. Having pleasure or being happy is to *feel* well. One may, of course, use the term *happiness* to connote something different, but in the way I use the term, one standard set of replies to the question 'How do you feel?' is 'I feel happy' or 'I feel unhappy.' The following set of answers would be rather awkward: 'I feel self-realized' or 'I do not feel self-realized.'

The most important feature of self-realization as compared with pleasure and happiness is its dependence upon a view of human capacities or, better, potentialities. This again implies a view of what human nature is. In practice, it does not imply a general doctrine of human nature. That is work for philosophical fields of research.

An individual whose attitudes are such that I would say that he or she takes self-realization as the ultimate or fundamental goal has to have a view of his or her nature and potentialities. The more they are realized, the more there is self-realization. The question 'How do you feel?' may be honestly answered in the positive or negative, whatever the level of self-realization. The question may, in principle, be answered in the negative, but like Spinoza, I think the valid answer is positive. The realization of fulfillment – using a somewhat less philosophical jargon – of the potentialities of oneself is *internally* related to happiness, but not in such a way that by *looking* for happiness, you will realize yourself. This is a clear point, incidentally, in John Stuart Mill's philosophy. You should not look hard for happiness. That is a bad way, even if you take, as Mill does, happiness as the ultimate or fundamental goal in life. I think that to look for self-realization is a better way. That is, to develop your capacities – using a rather dangerous word because the term *capacities* is easily interpreted in the direction of interpersonal, not intrapersonal, competition. But even the striving implied in the latter term may mislead. Dwelling in situations of intrinsic value, spontaneous nondirected awareness, relaxing from striving, is conducive to self-realization as I understand it. But there are, of course, infinite variations among humans according to cultural, social, and individual differences. This makes the key term *self-realization* abstract in its generality. But nothing more can be expected when the question is posed as it is: 'What might deserve to be called an ultimate or a fundamental goal?' We may reject the meaningfulness of such a question – I don't – but for us for whom it has meaning, the answer using few words is bound to be abstract and general.

Going back to the three key terms of pleasure, happiness, and self-realization, the third has the merit of being clearly and forcefully applicable to any being with a specific range of potentialities. I limit the range to living beings, using the word *living* in a rather broad sense. The terms *pleasure* and *happiness* are not so easily generalized. With the rather general concept of ecological self already introduced, the concept of self-realization naturally follows.

Let us consider the praying mantis, a formidable, voracious insect. These creatures have a nature fascinating to many people. Mating is part of their self-realization, but some males are eaten when performing the act of copulation. Is he happy; is he having pleasure? We don't know. Well done if he does! Actually, he feeds his partner so that she gets strong offspring. But it does not make sense to me to attribute happiness to these males. Self-realization, yes; happiness, no. I maintain the internal relationship between self-realization and happiness among people and among some animal groups. As a professional philosopher, I am tempted to add a point inspired by Zen Buddhism and Spinoza: Happiness is a feeling, yes, but the act of realizing a potential is always an interaction involving one single concrete unit, one gestalt, I would say, and three abstract aspects, subject, object, medium. What I said about joyfulness in nature holds for happiness in nature. We should not conceive them as merely subjective feelings.

The rich reality of the world is getting even richer through our specific human endowments; we are the first kind of living beings we know of who have the potential to live in community with all other living beings. It is our hope that all those potentialities will be realized – if not in the near future, then at least in the somewhat more remote future.

The Place of Joy in a World of Fact

The solution of environmental problems is presupposed in all utopias. For example, every family is to enjoy free nature under Marxian communism. 'In a communist society,' Marx says in a famous passage in *The German Ideology*, 'nobody has one exclusive sphere of activity but each can be accomplished in any branch he wishes. Society regulates the general production and thus makes it possible for me to do one thing today and another tomorrow: to hunt in the morning, fish in the afternoon, tend cattle in the evening, engage in literary criticism after dinner, just as I have in mind, without ever becoming a hunter, fisherman, shepherd, or critic.'

The complete individual is not a specialist; he or she is a generalist and an amateur. This does not mean that the person has no special interests, never works hard, or does not partake in the life of the community. The complete individual does so, however, from personal inclination, with joy, and within the framework of his or her value priorities.

In the future ideal society, whether outlined by Marx or by more bourgeois prophets, there will be people who might use most of their energy doing highly specialized, difficult things, but as amateurs – that is, from inclination and from a mature philosophy of life. There will be no fragmentary men and women, and certainly no fragmentary ecologists.

We all, I suppose, admire the pioneers who, through endless meetings held in contaminated city air, have succeeded in establishing wilderness areas in the United States. Unfortunately, their constant work in offices and corridors has largely ruined their capacity to enjoy these wilderness areas. They have lost the capacity to show, *in action*, what they care for; otherwise, they would spend much more time (and even live) in the wilderness. Many people verbally admire wilderness areas, but have not stepped down from their exalted positions, as chairs of this or that, to enjoy these areas at least part of the year.

What I say here about advocates of wilderness seems, unhappily, to be valid for advocates of a better environment in general. Ordinary people show a good deal of skepticism toward verbally declared values that are not expressed in the lifestyle of the propagandist. Environmentalists sometimes succumb to a joyless life that belies their concern for a better environment. This cult of dissatisfaction is apt to add to the already fairly advanced joylessness we find among socially responsible, successful people and to undermine one of the chief presuppositions of the ecological movement: that joy is related to the environment and to nature.

In short, the best way to promote a good cause is to provide a good example. One ought not to be afraid that the example will go unnoticed. For example, Albert Schweitzer hid himself in Africa, but his public relations prospered and so did the sale of his books.

So much for utopias. My next concern is with how to get nearer to our utopias. I shall take up only one aspect: the relation between personal lifestyle and teaching.

The Lifestyle of Environmentalists

Joy is contagious. If we only talk about the joys of a good environment, though, it is of little avail.

I know that many *have* turned their backs on more lucrative careers and a life of security, cultivating well-established sciences. This is not enough, however. Life should manifest the peaks of our value priorities. Working for a better environment is, after all, only of instrumental value. We remain on the level of techniques. What criterion shall we use to follow the lead of our personal priorities? We do have one that is underrated among conscientious, responsible people: joy.

Joy According to 'Pessimistic' Philosophers

Suppose someone openly adhered to the doctrine that there cannot be too much cheerfulness under any circumstances – even at a funeral. The sad truth is, I think, that he or she would be classified as shallow, cynical, disrespectful, irreligious, or mocking.

Søren Kierkegaard is an important figure here. He *seems* to take anguish, desperation, a sense of guilt, and suffering as the necessary, and sometimes even sufficient, condition of authentic living, but he also insists upon continuous joy as a condition of living. Whatever is done without joy is of no avail. 'At seventy thousand fathoms' depth,' you should be glad. At seventy thousand fathoms, one should retain 'a joyful mind.' He sometimes calls himself Hilarius, the one permeated with *hilaritas* (Latin for 'cheerfulness').

Dread is the technical existentialist word for the kind of anxiety that opens the way to a deeper understanding of life. According to Heidegger (another hero of modern pessimism), dread is not an isolated, negative sensation. The mind is in a complex state in which dread cannot exist without joy; that is, one who thinks he or she has the dread experience but lacks joy suffers from an illusion. Dread has an internal relation to joy.

Our problem is not that we lack high levels of integration (that is, that we are immature and therefore joyless), but rather that we glorify immaturity. Do the most influential philosophers of our time and culture represent high degrees of maturity and integration? I have in mind not only Heidegger, Sartre, Kierkegaard, and Wittgenstein, but also Marx and Nietzsche. Tentatively, I must answer no. There are lesser-known but perhaps more mature philosophers, like Jaspers and Whitehead.

Should the world's misery and the approaching ecocatastrophe make one sad? My point is that there is no good reason to feel sad about all this. According to the philosophies I am defending, such regret is a sign of immaturity, the immaturity of unconquered passiveness and lack of integration.

The remedy (or psychotherapy) against sadness caused by the world's misery is to do something about it. I shall refrain from mentioning Florence Nightingale, but let me note that Gandhi loved to care for, wash, and massage lepers; he simply enjoyed it. It is very common to find those who constantly deal with extreme misery to be more than usually cheerful. According to Spinoza, the power of an individual is infinitely small compared with that of the entire universe, so we must not expect to save the whole world. The main point – which is built into the basic conceptual framework of Spinoza's philosophy – is that of activeness. By interacting with extreme misery, one gains cheerfulness. This interaction need not be direct. Most of us can do more in indirect ways by using our privileged positions in rich societies.

There are clear reasons for us not to concentrate all our efforts directly on extreme miseries, but rather to attack the causes, conditions, and other factors indirectly contributing to this misery. And, just as important, we need to encourage the factors that directly cause or facilitate the emergence of active (and therefore cheerful) work to alleviate misery.

Behind the prevailing widespread passivity found throughout the world is a lot of despair and pessimism concerning our capacity to have a good time. We tend to enjoy ourselves (except during vacations) in a private world of thoughtlessness, well insulated from the great issues of the day.

One of the strangest and next-to-paradoxical theses of Spinoza (and of Thomas Aquinas and others) is that knowledge of evil, or of misery, is inadequate knowledge. In short, there is no such object, whereas there is something good to know. Evil is always an absence of something, a lack of something positive. Their theory of knowledge holds that objects of knowledge are always something. When you say that you see that the glass is transparent, what you see, for example, is a red rose behind the glass. You do not see the transparency, which is not an object of perception.

In any event, while I do not think that the positive nonexistence of evil things can be shown without a great deal of redefinition of words, I nevertheless do not consider this view totally ridiculous. Like so many other strange points of view in major philosophies, it has an appeal and points in the right direction without perhaps stating anything clearly in the 'scientific' sense.

Spinoza on Joy

Spinoza operates with three main concepts of joy and three of sorrow. *Laetitia, hilaritas*, and *titillatio* are the three Latin terms for the positive emotions of joy. Translations of these terms are, to a surprising degree, arbitrary, because their function in Spinoza's system can be discovered only by studying the complex total structure of his system. Isolating one concept from the others is not possible. Moreover, the system is more than the sum of its parts. From a strict, professional point of view, you must take it or leave it as a whole.

I translate *laetitia* as 'joy' – a generic term comprising several important subkinds of joy. The main classification of joy is *hilaritas* (cheerfulness) and *titillatio* (pleasurable excitement). *Hilaritas* is the serene thing, coloring the whole personality, or better, the whole world.

Spinoza defines *hilaritas* as a joy to which every part of the body contributes. It does not affect just a subgroup of functions of the organism, but every one, and therefore the totality of the organism. Spinoza contends that there cannot be too much *hilaritas*.

The other main kind of joy, *titillatio*, affects a subgroup of the parts of the body. If very narrowly based and strong, it dominates and thereby inhibits the other kinds of joy. Accordingly, there can be too much of it. Here Spinoza mentions love of money, sexual infatuation, and ambition. He also mentions other sources of joy that are all good in moderate degrees if they do not hamper and inhibit one another.

A second classification of joy is that derived from the contemplation of our own achievement, creativity, or – more broadly – activeness, and the joy derived from the contemplation of the causes of joy outside us. The first he calls satisfaction, or repose in ourselves (*acquiescentia in se ipso*); the other he calls *amor*. There can be too much of them, however, because they sometimes refer to parts, not to the whole.

According to Spinoza, what refers to the whole of the body also refers to the whole of the conscious mind and to the whole of the universe or, more generally, to the whole of Nature, insofar as we know it. This is understandable from Spinoza's so-called philosophy of identity, which proclaims the ultimate identity of thought and matter, and from his theory of knowledge, which relates all our knowledge of the world to interaction with the body – just as biologists tend to do today.

Lack of self-acceptance (*acquiescentia in se ipso*) accounts for much of the passivity displayed by an important sector of the public in environmental conflicts. Many people are on the right side, but few stand up in public meetings and declare how they, as private citizens, feel about the pollution in their neighborhoods. They do not have sufficient self-respect, respect for their own feelings, or faith in their own importance. But they themselves do not have to fight for the changes; it is only necessary that they state their feelings and positions in public. A small minority will then fight with joy – supported by that considerable sector of people.

The distinction between pervasive joy (covering all) and partial joy need not be considered an absolute dichotomy but rather one that exists in degrees. Joy may be more or less pervasive. Clearly, higher degrees of joy require high degrees of integration of the personality, and high degrees of such integration require intense cultivation of the personal aspect of interaction with the environment. It requires a firm grasp of what we call value priorities – which Spinoza would call reality priorities, because of his resolute location of value among 'objective' realities. Spinoza distinguishes degrees of realness and perfection. That which is perfect is complete. Integration of personality presupposes that we never act as mere functionaries or specialists but always as whole personalities conscious of our value priorities, and of the need to manifest those priorities in social direct action.

The specific thing to be learned from Spinoza and certain modern psychologists is, however, to integrate the value priorities themselves in the world. We tend to say 'the world of facts,' but the separation of value from facts is, itself, mainly due to an overestimation of certain scientific traditions stemming from Galileo. These traditions confuse the *instrumental* excellence of the mechanistic worldview with its properties as a whole philosophy. Spinoza was heavily influenced by mechanical models of matter, but he did not extend them to cover 'reality.' His reality was neither mechanical, value-neutral, nor value-empty.

This cleavage into two worlds – the world of fact and the world of values – can theoretically be overcome by placing, as Spinoza does, joys and other so-called subjective phenomena into a unified total field of realities. This, however, is too much to go into here. I am more concerned with the place of joy among our total experiences. The objectivist conception of value is important, though, in any discussion in which technocrats tend to dismiss cheerfulness in the environment as something 'merely subjective.'

Spinoza makes use of the following short, crisp, and paradoxical definition of joy (*laetitia*): 'Joy is man's transition from lesser to greater perfection.' Somewhat less categorically, he sometimes says that joy is the affect by which, or through which, we make the transition to greater perfection. Instead of 'perfection,' we may say 'integrity' or 'wholeness.'

Of central importance, in my view, is the difference between these formulations and subjectivist ones proclaiming that joy only *follows* or *accompanies* these transitions to greater perfection. For Spinoza, the relation between joy and an increase in perfection is an *intrinsic* one. That is, the two can be separated only conceptually, not in practice. Such a realistic view of joy suggests that joyfulness, like color, attaches to and forms part of objects, but, of course, changes with the medium and must be defined in terms of interaction with organisms. Joy is linked intrinsically to an increase in many things: perfection, power and virtue, freedom and rationality, activeness, the degree to which we are the cause of our own actions, and the degree to which our actions are understandable by reference to ourselves. Joy is thus a basic part of the conceptual structure of Spinoza's system.

An increase in power is an increase in the ability to carry out what we sincerely strive to do. Power does not presuppose that we coerce other people; a tyrant may be less powerful than some poor soul sitting in prison. This concept of power has a long tradition and should not be forgotten. What we strive to do is defined in relation to what actually happens; thus 'to save the world from pollution' is not something anyone strives to do, but is rather a kind of limited effort to save the things around us.

Cheerfulness (*hilaritas*) requires action of the whole integrated personality and is linked to a great increase in power. In the absence of joy, there is no increase of power, freedom, or self-determination. Thus, lack of joy should be taken seriously, especially among so-called responsible people furthering a good cause. The joy of work, like any other partial joy, can dominate and subdue other sources of joy to such an extent that the overall result is stagnation or even a decrease in power. In Spinoza's terminology, this means a loss of perfection or integration and increased difficulty in reaching a state of cheerfulness.

'To be happy' is often equated with enjoying oneself, laughing, or relaxing in the sense of being passive. Enjoying oneself by becoming intoxicated, which decreases the higher integrations of the nervous system, results in resignation. It means giving up the possibility of joyfulness of the whole person. Cheerfulness, in the Spinozistic sense, may not always be expressed in laughter or smiling, but in concentration, presentness, activeness.

The example of Buddha may illustrate my point. Buddha was an active person, but had great repose in himself (*acquiescentia in se ipso*). Long before he died, he is said to have reached Nirvana, which, properly interpreted within Mahayana Buddhism, involves supreme integration and liberation of the personality, implying bliss or (in the terminology of Spinoza) *hilaritas*. Research by F. Th. Stcherbatsky (1974) and others concerning the term *dukkha* (conventionally translated as 'pain') shows that so-called pessimistic Buddhism also has a doctrine of joy as a central aspect of reaching freedom in Nirvana.

One may say, somewhat loosely, that what we now lack in our technological age is repose in oneself. The conditions of modern life prevent the full development of the self-respect and self-esteem that are required to reach a stable high degree of *acquiescentia in se ipso* (the term *alienation*, incidentally, is related to the opposite of *in se*, namely, *in alio*, wherein we repose in something else, something outside ourselves, such as achievement in the eyes of others – we are 'other directed').

Humility, as defined by Spinoza, is sorrow resulting from the contemplation of one's own impotency, weakness, and helplessness. A feeling of sorrow always involves a decrease of perfection, virtue, or freedom. We can come to know adequately more potent things than ourselves. This gives us such joy because of our activeness in the very process of knowing them. The realization of our own potency, and our active relation to the more potent, result in joy. Thus, instead of humility (which is a kind of sorrow), we feel three kinds of joy: first, the joy resulting from the contemplation of our own power, however small, which gives us *acquiescentia in se ipso*, self-respect and contentedness; second, the joy resulting from increased personal, active knowledge of things greater than we are; and third, the joy resulting from active interaction, which, strictly speaking, defines us (as well as other objects or fragments) in the total field of reality (or in Nature, in Spinoza's terminology).

Adequate knowledge always has a joyful personal aspect because it reveals a power (never a weakness) in our personality. In Spinoza's words:

Therefore, if man, when he contemplates himself, perceives some kind of impotency in himself, it does not come from his understanding himself, but from his power of action being reduced . . . To the extent that man knows himself with true rationality, to that extent it is assumed that he understands his essence, that is, his power.

We say with some haughtiness that Spinoza belongs to the age of rationalism, to the pre-Freudian, pre-Hitler era. Nevertheless, Spinoza in many ways anticipated Freud, and his term *ratio* must not be translated into our term *rational* or *rationality* unless we immediately add that his *ratio* was more flexible and was internally related to emotion. Rational action for him is action involving absolutely maximal perspective – that is, where things are seen as fragments of total Nature – which is, of course, not what we tend to call rational today. Spinoza was not an intellectual in the sense of modern Anglo-American social science.

Pity and commiseration (*misericordia* and *commiseratio*) are not virtues for Spinoza, and even less so for Gandhi, although they may have some positive instrumental value. Spinoza says that 'commiseration, like shame, although it is not a virtue, is nevertheless good in so far as it shows that a desire for living honestly is present in the man who is possessed with shame, just as pain is called good in so far as it shows that the injured part has not yet putrefied.' A modest function, but nevertheless of instrumental value! Tersely, Spinoza adds that 'a man who lives according to the dictates of reason strives as much as possible to prevent himself from being touched by commiseration.' People who are crippled are among those who practically unanimously agree.

Commiseration is sorrow and therefore is, in itself, an evil. According to certain conventional morality, a duty should be carried out even if there is no joy. This suggests that we had better disregard our duties if we are not permeated with joy. I find this interpretation rather fanatical, however, except when one adds a kind of norm concerning the high priority of developing the *capacity* for joy. 'Alas! I cannot do my duty today because it does not fill me with joy. Better to escalate my efforts to experience joy!' Spinoza does not stress the remedy to the above situation – greater integration – but he presupposes it. The case of humility shows how *ratio* changes sorrows to joys: Spinozistic psychoanalysis tries to loosen up the mental cramps that cause unnecessary pain.

Freud worked with the tripartition of id, ego, and superego. The superego, through its main application in explaining neuroses, has a rather ugly reputation: It coerces the poor individual to try the impossible and then lets the person experience shame and humility when there is no success. In Spinoza's analysis, the *ratio* also functions as a kind of overseer, but its main function is rather one of consolation. It directs our attention to what we can do rather than to what we cannot, and eliminates feelings of necessary separation from others; it stresses the harmony of rational wills and of well-understood self-interests.

A major virtue of a system like Spinoza's is the extreme consistency and tenacity with which consequences, even the most paradoxical, are drawn from intuitively reasonable principles. It meets the requirements of clarity and logic of modern natural science. The system says to us: 'You do not like consequence number 101? But you admit it follows from a premise you had admitted. Then give up the premise. You do not want to give up the premise? Then you must give up the logic, the rules of inference you used to derive the consequence. You cannot give them up? But then you have to accept the consequence, the conclusion. You don't want to? Well, I suppose you don't want clarity and integration of your views and your personality.' The rationality of a total view like Spinoza's is perhaps the only form of rationality capable of breaking down the pseudorational thinking of the conservative technocracy that currently obstructs efforts to think in terms of the total biosphere and its continued blossoming in the near and distant future.

The Philosophical Premises of Environmentalism

Personally, I favor the kind of powerful premises represented in Chinese, Indian, Islamic, and Hebrew philosophy, as well as in Western philosophy – namely, those having as a slogan the so-called ultimate unity of all life. They do not hide the fact that big fish eat small ones, but stress the profound interdependence, the functional unity, of such a biospheric magnitude that nonviolence, mutual respect, and feelings of identification are always potentially there, even between the predator and its so-called victim. In many cultures, identification is not limited merely to other living things but also to the mineral world, which helps us conceive of ourselves as genuine surface fragments of our planet, fragments capable of somehow experiencing the existence of all other fragments: a microcosm of the macrocosm.

Another idea, right at the basis of a system from which environmental norms are derivable, is that of self-realization. The mature human individual, with a broadened self, acknowledges a right to self-realization that is universal. Consequently, he or she seeks a social order, or rather a biospheric order, that maximizes the potential for self-realization of all kinds of beings.

Level-headed, tough-minded environmentalists sometimes stress that it is sheer hypocrisy to pretend that we try to protect nature for its own sake. In reality, they say, we always have the needs of human beings in view. This is false, I think. Thousands of supporters of unpolluted so-called wastelands in northern Labrador wish simply that those lands should continue to exist as they are, for their own sake. The wastelands are of intrinsic, and not only instrumental, value. To invoke *specifically* human needs to describe this situation is misleading, just as it is misleading to say that it is egotistical to share one's birthday cake with others because one *likes* to share with others.

Self-realization is not a maximal realization of the coercive powers of the ego. The *self* in the kinds of philosophy I am alluding to is something expansive, and the environmental crisis may turn out to be of immense value for the further expansion of human consciousness.

In modern education, the difference between a world picture – or better, a world model – and a straightforward description of the world is glossed over. Atoms, particles, and wave functions are presented as parts or fragments of nature or are even presented as *the* real, objective nature, as contrasted with human projections into nature – the 'colorful' but subjective nature.

So-called physical reality, in terms of modern science, is perhaps only a piece of abstract mathematical reality – a reality we emphatically do not live in. Our living environment is made up of all the colorful, odor-filled, ugly, or beautiful details, and it is sheer folly to look for an existing thing without color, odor, or some other homely quality. The significance of this subject is a broad cultural one: the rehabilitation of the status of the immediately experienced world, the colorful and joyful world. *Where* is joy in the world of fact? Right at the center!

Lifestyle Trends Within the Deep Ecology Movement

The following list offers ways that supporters of the deep ecology movement can joyfully adapt their lifestyle to the movement.

1. Use simple means; avoid unnecessary, complicated instruments and other sorts of means.
2. Choose activities most directly serving values in themselves and having intrinsic value. Avoid activities that are merely auxiliary, have no intrinsic value, or are many states away from fundamental goals.
3. Practice anticonsumerism. This negative attitude follows from trends 1 and 2.
4. Try to maintain and increase the sensitivity and appreciation of goods in sufficient supply for all to enjoy.
5. Eliminate or lessen neophilia – the love of what is new merely because it is new.

6. Try to dwell in situations of intrinsic value and to act rather than being busy.

7. Appreciate ethnic and cultural differences among people; do not view the differences as threats.

8. Maintain concern about the situation in developing nations, and attempt to avoid a standard of living too much higher than that of the needy (maintain a global solidarity of lifestyle).

9. Appreciate lifestyles that can be maintained universally – lifestyles that are not blatantly impossible to sustain without injustice toward fellow humans or other species.

10. Seek depth and richness of experience rather than intensity.

11. Appreciate and choose, when possible, meaningful work rather than just making a living.

12. Lead a complex, not complicated, life, trying to realize as many aspects of positive experiences as possible within each time interval.

13. Cultivate life in community (*Gemeinschaft*) rather than in society (*Gesellschaft*).

14. Appreciate, or participate in, primary production – small-scale agriculture, forestry, fishing.

15. Try to satisfy vital needs rather than desires.
16. Attempt to live in nature rather than just visiting beautiful places; avoid tourism (but occasionally make use of tourist facilities).
17. When in vulnerable nature, live 'light and traceless.'
18. Appreciate all life-forms rather than merely those considered beautiful, remarkable, or narrowly useful.
19. Never use life-forms merely as means. Remain conscious of their intrinsic value and dignity, even when using them as resources.
20. When there is a conflict between the interests of dogs and cats (and other pet animals) and wild species, try to protect the wild creatures.
21. Try to protect local ecosystems, not only individual life-forms, and think of one's own community as part of the ecosystems.
22. Besides deploring the excessive interference in nature as unnecessary, unreasonable, and disrespectful, condemn it as insolent, atrocious, outrageous, and criminal – without condemning the people responsible for the interference.

23. Try to act resolute and without cowardice in conflicts, but remain nonviolent in words and deeds.
24. Take part in or support nonviolent direct action when other ways of action fail.
25. Practice vegetarianism.

Industrial Society, Postmodernity, and Ecological Sustainability

The Human Condition

It is a trait that belongs to human beings, and only human beings as far as we know, to try to make a kind of survey of their existence, to sort out what is of primary value and what they regard more or less with indifference; what they need and what are just whimsical wishes.

On their way to decreasing their own whimsicality and thoughtlessness, people in industrial societies like to learn about the problems that other people in other cultures have grappled with. This leads inevitably to rather broad and general talk, not just *small narratives* – a much-cherished term in deconstructive postmodernist literature. It leads to investigations that are immense in their breadth of perspective and to results that are always open to doubt and correction.

What follows reflects some thoughts by two sorts

of human beings, those who for many years lived in a nonindustrial country and those who have spent many years together with tiny living creatures in grand mountains. Both sorts are, in a sense, products of modern Western industrial societies – but not mere products. Because the reflections cover a vast terrain, they lack the elaboration and concreteness that we need in our attempts to understand and modify our behavior in concrete situations.

Comparing nonindustrial with industrial societies, including the fate of local communities, one sees that many of the nonindustrialized societies have shown a continuity and strength that the industrialized societies cannot hope to achieve, because industrial societies are unsustainable ecologically. Industrialized societies also seem unable to stop ethical erosion and increased criminality, including those in the fifteen to twenty-three-year-old age group.

Surveying the situation today, one sees also that the attraction of the industrial societies' *material* richness and technical acumen is overwhelming even the very young people in nonindustrial societies. This situation is tragic for at least two reasons. First, it would be ecologically catastrophic to have five billion people behaving as people in the industrial societies behave. Second, it is unrealistic to expect that substantial increases in material affluence can be reached in non-industrial societies without unacceptable levels of criminality and the erosion of feelings of fellowship and mutual dependence.

Using the term *modern* to relate to the emergence of the culture of the industrial countries, one may still hope that today's nonindustrial societies will experience *a development from premodern to postmodern* cultures. The development of the industrial societies has brought humanity into a blind alley. The postmodern state of affairs implies the satisfaction of the vital economic needs of the total population, but not affluence. The key slogan would be 'Enough is enough.' When vital economic needs are satisfied, there is *enough* in terms of material richness. Of course, there are other forms of richness – in principle, limitless richness.

The near future of the industrial countries, let us say, the period until 2050, should emphasize a reduction in the use of energy and in material production, until the countries reach a level attainable by the total human population without the danger of gigantic catastrophes. The next step would be to reach *full* ecological sustainability.

In the years after World War II, a mighty slogan asked for a vast increase (mostly material) in production. When production and productivity in the richest countries soared as never before, a new powerful slogan appeared: 'Consume! Consume!' because of overproduction. Today, this reason is replaced by an appeal to consume to overcome unemployment. The notorious appeal of the retail analyst Victor Lebow promoted consumption to relieve overproduction, but otherwise, the appeal provides an amusing picture of the strange sort of economy prevalent in the highly industrialized countries: 'Our enormously productive economy . . . demands that we make consumption our way of life, that we convert the buying and use of goods into rituals, that we seek our spiritual satisfaction, our ego satisfaction, in consumption . . . we need things consumed, burnt up, worn out, replaced, and discarded at an ever increasing rate.'

The contribution to the ecological crisis by a minority of half a billion people has been such that an acceptable level of interference in the ecosystems by ten times as many people must be very much smaller per half billion. In the near future, 'the total unecological product' created yearly by the industrial countries should be at such a level that, multiplied by ten, it would not point toward gigantic catastrophes. If we call the per-capita sum total of unecological consequences by production for a given community or country ΣP_u and that of consumption ΣC_u and the number of people in the community or country N, the total unecological consequences of policies ΣU may be put into a form looking like an equation:

$$\Sigma U = (\Sigma P_u + \Sigma C_u) \times N$$

The ΣU may represent a local community, a region, a country, or that of humanity in general.

For industrial societies, their ΣU_I should not be greater than 10 percent of the total ΣU_T. Without substantial progress toward that goal occurring each year in the industrial societies, this will be difficult to accomplish.

As a firm supporter of the deep ecology movement, I hold that a decrease in consumption and a slow decrease in population will *not* necessarily result in a decrease in the quality of life. There will be a transition period, during which some people living according to the slogan 'Enough is never enough' will have difficulties. But provided the downscaling is effectuated with a strong sense of justice, major uprisings may not occur.

It is an indication of a narrow time perspective when people reject the idea of a slow decrease in population because there will be too many old, unproductive people compared with younger, productive ones. The undesired ratio will make itself felt only for a short transition period, and the perspective we need covers hundreds of years.

Disrespect of One's Own Nonindustrial Cultures

Since World War II, the general *Western* disrespect for nonindustrial cultures has changed into a deep and serious respect among an increasing minority. In the same period, disrespect in the nonindustrial cultures of *their* own culture seems to have increased formidably, especially among the young. Among the factors contributing to this are an equally formidable increase in tourism and smart sales campaigns.

Depreciation is often expressed in front of representatives of the West. In Beding and other Sherpa communities of Garwal Himalaya, monks had libraries of old Tibetan scripts, for example, prayers directed to Tseringma ('the long good life's mother'), a formidable 7,146-meter-high peak directly above the village. In the 1950s and 1960s, the villagers showed reluctance to admit that they had such things. People hid such documents as shameful signs of backwardness. They were ashamed of their tradition of a cult of holy mountains going back many hundreds (or thousands?) of years. Their daily prayers to the mountain were beautifully written down and, until the twentieth century, regarded as treasures. How were scholars able to obtain such old documents? By buying them? No – by living among the families and showing *respect*. Then they could get the old scrolls as gifts. Otherwise, the scrolls might be destroyed.

Depreciation of one's own local or regional culture may be a worldwide phenomenon among young people, but nothing known in human history can be compared to what is happening in our time. Traditional cultures everywhere are under severe pressure – mostly with fatal results.

Disrespect of one's own culture includes disrespect of the land. In the Beding area and other Sherpa areas of Nepal, the forest was respected and no living trees were cut down for fuel. Each tree was looked upon as something that had its own life, it own interest, its own dignity. With the breakdown of customs, this deep ecology attitude vanished. The enormous mountaineering expeditions increased the mobility of the Sherpas, who were hired by the thousands to carry water – and often to heat it using wood – for daily hot showers for the sahibs. These practices generated completely different attitudes toward mountains and forests: disrespect of holiness, purely instrumental attitudes toward timber, wood, and fuel. Deforestation above 9,000 feet began in earnest. Without trees as cover, erosion started on a grand scale. Today, practically nothing is left. Nepal became an 'export country,' exporting hundreds of millions of tons of soil to India. The rivers brought much of the soil to the giant Indian dams, built largely through misguided efforts at 'development,' and became filled with silt.

With no cultural restraints and little Western scientific knowledge, the destruction of Nepal gradually reached gigantic proportions. Immigration from the countryside to the city of Kathmandu accelerated. The young were not willing to walk all day for fuel. They would rather live without dignity in Kathmandu.

A young, exceptionally gifted Sherpa who had been with many expeditions got the opportunity to start a sports shop in Canada, but he returned to his own country after a while. He expressed in a few words his reason for going back: 'Here we enjoy peace with ourselves.' So many of the people he met on expeditions and in Canada, evidently, had no peace within themselves. They wished to be different from what they were; they worked hard to develop, achieve, succeed, and be better. They could not let time flow. Unfortunately, very few young people have the necessary faculty of *independent* judgment, nor do they have the opportunity to compare the Western quality of life with their own in their 'poor' countries. I am not referring here to the half billion people in nonindustrial countries who are desperately poor, who lack the most basic means to live a decent life.

Western Belief That We Project Personal Traits onto Natural Objects

In traditional, nonindustrial societies, we find more and stronger 'personification' of natural forces and nonhuman living beings. The tendency to personify is often said to be archaic, meaning that it precedes the great religions and cultures. The term *anthropomorphism* is often used in a pejorative sense for the erroneous attribution of specifically human traits to entities that are not human or not even capable of sense experience. Before starting to drink beer together, the Sherpas threw a little beer in the direction of Tseringma – beer for *her*.

If a big mountain precipice may be spontaneously experienced as dark and evil, it *is*, in an important sense, dark and evil. If this experience motivates us in the West to throw a stone at the mountain as a punishment for being evil, we have succumbed to a mistake. In a nonindustrial culture, throwing beer or a stone is meaningful – or was meaningful – but not within *our* conceptual framework.

Animals, plants, and some nonliving things may be experienced as evil or good. They may be experienced as arrogant, proud, insolent, and self-domineering or humble, sheepish, crestfallen, and so on. Education in industrial countries is strongly centered on a subject-object cleavage: Some traits of animals are real and objective attributes; others are said to be *projected* onto the animals. The latter traits are merely subjective.

In practical life, the distinction is a plus, but it downplays spontaneous experience with its richness, intensity, and depth. It favors thinking in terms of abstract relations and structures of reality, not in terms of content. When we depart and decide to meet again on a mountain, the mountain must be defined in terms of our society and culture, defined as an *object* we have in common. This, however, does not identify the mountain as an object 'in itself.'

Our vast abstractions are momentous cultural achievements specific to Western culture. Contemporary mathematical physics is an example. Here the link to spontaneous experience is extremely indirect and spotty, but strong because of the high level of mathematical deduction. Because of its severe limitation of modeling abstract structure, it expresses an intercultural type of knowledge, that is, intercultural if one does not rely on popularization but sticks to the severe mathematical form of what is asserted. In that case, the cultural background disappears! The equations are intercultural, but any *interpretations* in terms we are acquainted with in our daily life depend on specific cultures. Communication among experts is compatible with deep cultural differences among the participants.

There is no physical *world* with specifically physical *content*. There is a reality, the content of which we have direct contact with only through and in our spontaneous experiences. It is a reality of infinite richness.

No dichotomies of fundamental character seem adequate to describe it. Distinctions between physical and mental 'worlds,' or between subjective and object-ive worlds, are not adequate for describing reality. The philosophical reaction against taking the latter distinction as fundamental has increased in strength since the 1890s. Should we, mused A. N. Whitehead, stop admiring the beauty of a rose and instead admire the poet who admirably sings about it? Would not that be reasonable if the rose *in itself* is neither beautiful nor ugly? Is there 'objectivity' only in electrons and similar colorless items? The beauty of the rose itself is spontaneously experienced and is as real as anything can be.

Western Schools and European Unity

The school systems of the industrial states are all adapted to the common, very special way of life in those states. Unawareness of this limitation discourages reforms that would widen the perspective; consequently, the schools remain provincial.

A major concern in schools that attempt less one-sided perspectives is for the future of the children: How will they get jobs when their knowledge does not fit in with the established order? If the parents are economically rich, they can help the youngsters get along in the unique and strange world of the industrial growth societies, in spite of their 'far out' schooling – but otherwise, the young tend to get into trouble. Therefore, educators often give up the most radical sorts of reforms.

Let us look at some of the curricula children now have to learn, starting with mathematics. Mathematical instruction today is completely Westernized and utilitarian, reflecting the typical Western emphasis on proof. There is no trace of Chinese or Indian old mathematical culture. Little is taught about bold mathematical conjectures such as those in number theory; little is taught about endless fractions and orders of the infinite. With more adequate education in mathematics, children are encouraged to love the subject and tend to continue to relish it after leaving school. Mathematics in itself is an ecologically very innocent hobby! Masses of excellent paper are wasted every day in schools, but some could be used to design geometrically interesting buildings.

Proper mathematics should, of course, not lack instruction about the existence of proofs and, in later years, of axiomatic or formal systems in general – but only basic notions, 'axiomatic thinking,' not complicated applications. Perhaps three or four different proofs of the Pythagorean Theorem and a couple of other simple proofs would suffice to help students understand the miracle of proofs and – later – allow them to grasp the *essentials* of deductive systems.

What about chemistry? Children love to play with (more or less) harmless chemicals. Let them see miracles, such as how two colorless liquids, brought together, may create fantastic colors! In organic chemistry, they may learn about the long series like CH_4, C_2H_5, and C_3H_8, . . . , and enjoy building molecules. Isomers of C_4H_{10}! Very inexpensive and elegant colored tools are available today. They may learn about colors used by Rembrandt and others. Children appreciate crystals, and with a magnifying glass, they may enjoy learning about some of the most beautiful forms. They can combine this with some mineralogy and petrology: the joy of finding stones, learning to enjoy natural things, of which there are enough for all. At the university level, there should be an opportunity to go deeply into modern, theoretical 'hard' chemistry.

Let me now mention history. A major guideline is to focus on the local (bioregional) and the global, with less emphasis on the national. There should be more about interlocal movements, less about internationalism, more emphasis on cultural diversity and the Fourth World.

The distinction between global and international is important for many reasons. One of them is that few nations have much power, while the great global corporations have more than most nations, shaping economic life everywhere.

It has now been more than half a century since the school textbooks of the Scandinavian countries were 'adjusted' to be compatible with one another.

Until then, a war between them was, as a matter of habit, described systematically, with each participant reporting and ethically judging what happened according to that participant's own extremely one-sided propaganda.

There is no hope of establishing peaceful, green societies as long as conflicts are described in a way that fosters prejudice and hatred. Equally pernicious is the underestimation of social and political calamities attributable to the destruction of one's own land. The tentative *history* of ecological calamities is now available, and the material should be integrated into school textbooks.

Until recently, 'world history' for children – at least in Europe – has been atrociously anthropocentric. The history of the planet and of life should be in focus as part of the global perspective. The history of bioregions takes care of the local perspective.

Social and cultural anthropology cannot be completely absorbed into textbooks of history, but there is room for some material on these subjects. The outlook of economic anthropology is relevant: Children should know that the economic system they are part of in the West is an extremely special kind. In the long view, general cultural and, especially, religious institutions have been stronger in comparison with the economic. In the industrial countries, the history of capitalism since the fifteenth century tells us a lot about our successes and our failures.

Here is not the place to go through the curriculum of schools and colleges. Wide differences of approach are needed, but the state of affairs today is deplorable: Pupils aged six to sixteen (what I call children herein) in the rich industrial societies are generally imbued with ways of thinking adapted to a kind of society that, hopefully, will disappear in their own lifetime.

As has always been the case, though, schools mirror society, and the transition to green societies must occur simultaneously at many sections of the long frontier of change.

As they learn history in the schools of the future, our children and grandchildren may be confronted with sentences like the following: 'The productivity of industry and agriculture increased exponentially in the richest industrial countries in the last half of the twentieth and early twenty-first centuries. A wild consumerism not only threatened the conditions of life on our planet, but also was accompanied by an impoverishment of relations between people, a degradation of fellowship, and an increase of asocial attitudes. (New phenomenon: criminal careers for children between eight and sixteen years of age.) The economy of a country was not expected to adapt to its culture, but the culture to the economy.'

People in the developing countries do not seem to realize that the consumerism of the West is doomed. They have no chance to see that there is no future for the kind of life they observe the tourists living. Here is one of the great challenges in the years to come. What can be done to change the picture those people have of our common future? What can be done to assist a transition from the preindustrial to the postindustrial?

A combined focus on the local and the global is impossible under conditions of *economic* globalization, as the latter term is now used. *Economic globalization* is somewhat misleading. A better term might be *globalization of the four freedoms*, referring to the so-called four freedoms of the Treaty of Rome, which was the basis for the European Common Market and *is still* at the core of the present-day European Union (EU). The document's style of globalization implies successive expansion of its 'four freedoms' until it also covers trade among the three giants, the European Union, the United States (and Canada), and Japan, and reluctantly over the rest of the globe. The term *four freedoms* refers to the free (duty-free) crossing of goods and materials through borders, the free flow of services, the freedom to compete for jobs anywhere (people), and the freedom of capital to flow across any borders. The four freedoms *imply four prohibitions*, the violation of which will be punished by the authorities. Namely, the freedoms involve strong, adequate *protection* – for social, medical, ecological, or other reasons of cultural relevance – against the import of certain goods or services, or against certain kinds of flow of foreign capital into a local, regional, or any other limited area, for example, the Arctic coast of Norway.

Representatives of the EU tempted politicians and the public in the four new countries that in 1994 had expressed a wish to join by emphasizing transition periods with less strict negative rules. In the long run, though, the overall tendency is to prepare for tighter and tighter economic unions – like that of the United States. The outlook is a world of *consumers* getting more products more cheaply than ever before through wider mobility. The only diversity of cultures here is one compatible with the supreme rules of a free world market!

Norway is the only Nordic country with family farms, and there is a definite agriculture, not just agribusiness. To protect this culture and to make it economically possible for its practitioners to survive, Norway 'subsidizes' its agriculture. That is, there is a *transfer of income* so that the farmers can offer the public their products at low prices, prices that are not high enough to cover farm expenses. In an important sense, it is not the farmer, but the public, that is subsidized and protected against further increases of urbanized youth. The public has to pay more for milk, bread, and other agricultural commodities than it would on the *world market*. We are asked to destroy the farm culture in favor of city culture.

The Norwegian market today is not completely a part of the cheap world market. Nevertheless, what Norwegians pay for their food is absurdly little, usually about 15 percent of their average income. That is, expenses for transportation (private car, etc.) and other goods are much greater. We must expect that in future green societies, food calculated as a percentage of income will cost us substantially more than it does today. One may say that on average, today's cost to satisfy vital *needs* is only a small fraction of the cost of satisfying *wants* – or to be more exact, a small fraction of the cost of satisfying wants that are 'normal' in the rich industrial countries. The economy of Norway is capitalist, but closer to a mixed economy than that of, say, the United States.

One may, very roughly, class as a mixed economy an economic system with a free market within a framework that permits fairly strong rules governing the operation of the market. Such rules make Norway, for example, capable of protecting certain activities – agricultural, industrial, and others – from foreign competition and, ultimately, from the world market. The government has recently said yes to a new round of the General Agreement on Tariffs and Trade (GATT), and this turns Norway into a more stream-lined capitalist country, distancing itself from the ideals of a mixed economy. (Unhappily, the term *mixed economy* is sometimes used for any capitalist system having one or more rules protecting the environment. This makes the United States and every other industrial state mixed-economy countries. It is hoped that this erosion of the terminology will not continue.)

What is the current status of efforts to promote green economies in relation to all this? If a country can sell products more cheaply than certain others because it has a higher degree of irresponsible ecological policy, the four freedoms prevent the more responsible countries from keeping the products out. Consumers cannot be expected to keep track of the ecological atrocities in other countries. It is therefore unlikely that a green economy, at least in the near future, will suddenly be established in a single country. In the short run, countries with the most irresponsible policies will profit from export, but in the long run, other states will presumably introduce economic sanctions in favor of their own exports.

From the viewpoint of the Treaty of Rome, the individuality, or 'personality,' of local economic activity cannot be ideal, because of the lack of fierce competition and the failure to emphasize maximization of profits. The machinery of economic activity as conceived by supporters of the Treaty of Rome is taken to be universalizable, common to all possible cultures. That is, the introduction may always take place, and it will change the culture. This way of describing the treaty is, however, too simple for serious debate. Minor differences in an economic system may be tolerated, even supported – for example, because a difference favors tourism or because a difference belongs to the simple cultural traits of which the population is particularly proud.

At the moment, applicants for membership in the European Union will, as mentioned, be permitted to continue *for a time* particular activities inconsistent with the Treaty of Rome. The time is mostly longer than the interval between political elections. This makes it easier for particular governments to join the EU because many negative and controversial consequences of membership will not manifest themselves until after the government's time in power.

In concluding, I admit that centralization of power today is furthered by a greater number of benevolent people than ever before – people and institutions interested in fostering more trade, in letting people consume and travel more than ever. Until recently, it was widely held that capitalist competition leads to war. Today, it may lead instead to systems of tacit and explicit agreement between corporations in order to keep this system from failing. In Japan and the United States, the consensus is that wars of trade between the two giants are not, in the long run, in the interest of industry. The preferred situation, it is said, is for both to have a free market comprising Japan, the United States, and Europe, but with the leaders of the corporations forming mutual agreements aimed at avoiding undesirable kinds of competition. We might end up with a culture, including education, that is adapted to the world market rather than the other way around. Because of the central idea of 'the more trade, the better,' combined with a vastly increased mobility of people and goods, ecological problems can only increase.

Our Way is Back to Sustainability, Not to Old Forms of Society

It is tempting to see 'us' – members of the rich industrial countries – as 'moderns,' more or less disregarding nine-tenths of humanity. This major portion of humans also live today; they belong to the contemporary scene, but are considered relics of the past.

As to the exact delimitation of modernity in terms of age, one proposal is to think of the time from the European Renaissance to the present; another proposal is to include only the period from the start of the industrial revolution, covering about two centuries at least. Not without some arrogance, many of us now look forward to the creation of 'postindustrial' societies.

The following reflections, colored by personal experiences, result from an urge to examine industrial society in the light of values established in nonindustrial, 'traditional' societies and in light of lifeways that are ecologically fully sustainable. Such has been the life of human beings for long periods. Alaska was inhabited for thousands of years by people with ecologically sustainable, diverse cultures. In Norway, people followed the retreat of the ice eight thousand years ago. As soon as reindeer could prosper, human beings prospered.

Ecological sustainability was only one characteristic of traditional societies, and it did somewhat reflect the small numbers of people. Many of those societies we would class as ecologically unsustainable if they had had millions of members. The reindeer-based, very loose societies were dependent to some extent upon the ratio between the number of reindeer and the number of human beings.

Of course, there is 'no way back' in general, but it is important to remember that global unsustainability is something very new and that for a wide variety of stable cultures, our planet was a tremendously big, rich, eminently hospitable, and benign world. Difficulties had to arise only when human beings pressed away other human beings from the areas where life was easiest, or at least not a greater challenge than desired.

It is to be hoped that an ever-increasing minority

will view unsustainability as an undignified, stupid – if not plainly ridiculous – state of affairs. One also hopes that an increasing minority will express this attitude with increasing boldness – but without arrogance, since few activists can avoid making use of the facilities offered in the industrial societies.

In short, there is no way back to societies that belong to the past, but there is a way back to ecological sustainability. In fact, there is not just one way but many ways, so that widely different, sustainable cultures are possible. Valuable contributions to the study of these ways are not lacking, but they are mostly unknown to the public. Unavoidably, large segments of the public have the feeling that 'environmentalists' want to turn back time. When some of these enthusiasts announce, 'Back to the Pleistocene!' the suspicion is well-founded. The indication of ways to go does not, of course, amount to elaborate plans and blueprints. Such absence of detail has been the rule, not the exception, in all new major human undertakings. It has never stopped those who have the proper motivation to work for change.

There are not only rough plans of how to solve some of the most serious ecological problems, but also even tentative – very tentative – estimates of the costs in money and labor. A dollar estimate was published in *State of the World, 1988*. An updated 1994 rough estimate could be – let us say – $250 billion annually. Here I shall only mention some theoretical aspects of such an estimate.

Owing to the current lack of institutional infrastructure necessary to use such a large sum rationally, the $250-billion-per-year expenditure may not be reached until ten years from now, that is, from 2005 onward. The sum, both in money *and in work*, would be paid almost entirely by the rich countries. The vast activity *within* the rich countries in preparation for the undertaking would demand workers in great numbers with a great variety of skills. Given present levels of unemployment, there is no doubt that the necessary number could be mobilized. Production, in the wide sense of theoretical economics, would increase. It would be registered as increased gross domestic product (GDP).

The undertaking, mostly done by the people in non-industrial countries, but in close cooperation with people from the industrial countries, would be accomplished only through the substantial mobilization of people and capital. As an example, consider reforestation. Today, several hundred million people lack fuel for cooking their food or cleaning their drinking water – the distance to the nearest wood is simply too far. Under such circumstances, planted trees are normally used for fuel as soon as they reach the size of bushes. Therefore, the people must be offered other kinds of fuel for at least twenty years. Even then, a great number of honest people must act as protectors of the growing plants. In short, reforestation is a *socially* complex, labor-intensive undertaking, and the economics of both the industrial and the nonindustrial countries would be greatly stimulated by reforestation.

Inevitably, the consumption, not the production, of the rich countries would decrease. The increased consumption would come from the nonindustrial countries and would not interfere with the increased GDP in rich countries. GDP is *not* a measure of domestic consumption, as is often thought. If Norway produces a thousand tiny hydroelectric plants for use in poor countries, it decreases its unemployment and reduces poverty among others.

Global reforestation will not, of course, mean complete reforestation, but reforestation insofar as it both ensures ecological sustainability and meets the vital needs of the people. As already mentioned, however, the change would start out slowly, even if money and a workforce were available. It is not like mobilizing in times of war in a country whose military institutions have been prepared well in advance. Large-scale rational and ethically responsible reforestation is a new sort of undertaking that requires highly educated, corruption-resistant people. It will take a long time. One generation? Three generations? Nobody knows. There is, however, no point of no return. Compared with the investment of life, work, and money in a great war, the investment needed to overcome the ecological crisis is very small. Moreover, the work of a determined minority could get the work started in earnest.